Little Book of

Good Words

Motivational, Funny, Insightful Quotes

Mark Turner

Copyright © 2023
Frisco, Texas

Tribute Publishing

Little Book of Good Words
First Edition June 2023

All Worldwide Rights Reserved
ISBN: 978-1-7337727-7-8

All Rights Reserved. No part of this book may be reproduced, stored in a retrieval system, or transmitted, in any form, or by any means, electronic, recorded, photocopied, or otherwise, without the prior written permission of the copyright owner, except by a reviewer who may quote brief passages in a review.

Printed in the United States of America

Introduction

I am often asked to share my favorite quote or saying. Mike Rodriguez, one of my best friends in the world, God rest his soul, used to say, "Mark, you need to write one of these books of sayings. You are filled with Mark-isms."

Rick Ferguson, another one of my best friends, has encouraged me often to write as well.

Each of us has a unique story to tell, a personal journey filled with joys and sorrows, triumphs and challenges, and the lessons we have learned along the way. And within each of these experiences lies a nugget of wisdom, a profound truth, or an inspiring thought that can guide us and motivate us to be the best version of ourselves.

In this book of quotes that I love so dearly, I invite you to join me on a journey through my own experiences and the insights that have shaped my life.

These quotes are reflections of my thoughts, feelings, and beliefs, gathered from different moments in my life.

They are a product of my own struggles, successes, humor and everything in between.

I hope that by sharing these words with you, they will bring a sense of connection and inspiration to your own journey.

My hope is that these quotes will encourage you to reflect on your own experiences, find meaning in your own challenges, and embrace the opportunities for growth and transformation that life offers us.
Ultimately, this book is an invitation to explore the power of personal reflection and

to discover the wisdom that lies within each of us. So let us embark on this journey together and see where our own personal quotes can take us.

So folks, here is a Little Book of Good Words for everyone to enjoy.

My prayer is that something within one of these will resonate with you and your life will be changed.

God Bless each of you richly and often,

Mark Turner
GROW ON!

**Your mind is a garden,
Your thoughts are the seeds,
You can grow flowers,
Or you can grow weeds.**

You are responsible for the direction of your life. You are where you are, and you are who you are because of what has gone into your mind. You have what you have because of the decisions you have made.

If you don't like where you find yourself, change. We are not trees! We can move, we can alter, we can CHANGE.

The fastest method to change is feeding your mind with something that sows greatness into your soul.

When someone doesn't value your words, SILENCE Is the answer!

Sometimes the best method of communication is silence. We live in a world today where the "spin doctors" dissect every word and apply their own meaning.

When in doubt about speaking, take a pause and choose silence.

If we don't start, we certainly can't arrive.

You don't have to be great to start, but you have to start to be great.

Many in life dream, think, plan, hope, wish and pray. However, without ACTION, nothing happens.

Without action, dreams will remain dreams, plans simply remain plans, hope goes unfulfilled along with those wishes and many times prayers seem to go unanswered.

You can't back up to the stove of life and ask for heat if you haven't put any wood on the fire.

You can't control everything life has to throw at you every day. However, you can control the attitude that you will apply to each.

Life throws us curves all the time. While approaching the curve, a positive attitude will determine whether or not that curve is just a bend or a break.

Zig Ziglar said, "Positive thinking won't make everything better, but it will make everything better than negative thinking will."

To respond is Positive.

To react is Negative.

When the Doctor comes to you
and says you are having a reaction to the
medicine you have been prescribed,
we shudder.

When the Doctor comes to you and says
you are responding to the medicine
you have been prescribed,
you immediately feel better.

Strive to respond, not react.

**It amazes me how much
EXERCISE
and
EXTRA FRIES
Sound alike**

I love this one. Rick Ferguson has a saying,
"I can pass up everything but temptation."

I love fries. However, having
fries every day, compounded over time
will increase the waistline.

Let's keep our physical bodies
as healthy as we can.

**It's either
DAY ONE
or
"ONE DAY"
The choice is yours.**

Choose to start a path to better yourself.
Choose to read a book. Choose to listen to
an audio that inspires. Choose to attend a
seminar that feeds your life.

The time to choose is now.
Day 1.

Be where your feet are!

Put down the cell phone. Shut off all
electronic devices and focus
on those around you.

A story was published regarding people
visiting the Grand Canyon. As they all sat
on benches looking at their cell phones
and the pictures they had taken, the vast
expanse and beauty lay before them.

**Common sense is like deodorant.
Those that need it the most never use it.**

Life is simple. People make it hard.
Not using common sense makes it harder.

Take a breath. Stop and think before you act.

**You can't climb
the ladder to success
with your hands
in your pockets.**

Nothing beats good ole' fashioned work.
There is no elevator to the top
of the hill, only steps.

Successful people know that
each day they must climb the steps.
They must put forth the effort.

Three phases of life:

Go – Go
Slow – Go
No – Go

Oh, the vigor of being young. I remember I could go, go, go. Now that the calendar has slipped behind me, I find myself in the slow-go lane.

No matter which lane you are in, show gratitude and plant seeds of greatness in everyone you meet.

Make a decision.

**The road of life
is littered with flat squirrels
who couldn't make a decision.**

Nothing frustrates me more than indecision. We have to understand that no decision is an absolute decision as time marches forward.

You have a say…. make a decision….NOW.

You go where you LOOK.

Simple but very profound. When you focus on what you don't have, what you don't want, and what you have missed out on, you miss out on the things you could have and the things you want.

Your mind will multiply whatever it is fed or sees. Look toward excellence. Look toward service. Look to blessings.

Don't be so thirsty for opportunity that you drink from every cup handed to you... That's how you get poisoned!

Be patient. Be diligent. Take your time when presented with an opportunity.

Do your homework. Seek wise counsel.

**Don't blame a clown for acting like a clown.
Ask yourself why you keep going to the circus.**

You know those folks. The drama generators. The "always acting up" crowd.

Do your best to avoid them altogether.
If you keep going to the circus,
you will be part of the act.

If you want to buy things without looking at the price, you have to be able to work without looking at the clock.

A great work ethic will set you apart from the crowd in every endeavor you undertake.

Show up early, stay late.

Don't be a clock watcher, be a career maker.

No pressure.

No diamonds.

The best things come after applying some pressure. Diamonds are no exception.

When you encounter the stresses of life, know that they are shaping you into the diamond you were intended to be.

Some people are like splinters.

They will cause you pain until you remove them.

Negative people have a tendency to rub off on everyone they come in contact with.

Critical people have a way of turning every opportunity into a problem.

Surround yourself with positive thinkers, great minds and excellence seekers.

**Sometimes you make
the right decision.
Sometimes you make
the decision right.**

Simply making a decision is the first step.
Sometimes, after making the decision,
the best course of success is to work
to make the decision right.

Don't be afraid to make a decision.
No decision is a decision
as time marches forward.

**To become significant in people's eyes,
you must make a difference in people's lives.**

People will follow you and people
will love you when they know
you truly care about them.

A leader will invest his time in
growing his people and making
a difference in their lives.

Speak in such a way that others love to listen to you.

Listen in such a way that others love to speak to you.

Nothing is more compelling than to have someone listen to you. To do that, you must speak in a manner they understand. This is planting seeds of greatness within them.

When someone is talking to you, put the cell phone down. Stop, focus, LISTEN.

Beware of the thief that is after your purse.

But also beware of the thief that is after your promise.

Watch out for the thief that will steal your dreams. This thief can take many shapes – TV, hobbies, sleep, alcohol, drugs.

Perhaps one of the most egregious thieves is the one that tells you that you aren't enough.

**It's better to walk alone
than with a crowd
going in the wrong direction.**

Make sure you are walking your path
and that your path is one of
honesty and integrity.

Too many get swallowed up in the crowd
and swept along with them. Stand Out!

Sometimes you win.

Sometimes you learn.

Failure is only that if you don't learn.

Simply because something did not go your way, or you did not take the blue ribbon does not constitute failure.

Failure only occurs when, after the battle is over, nothing has been learned.

Your input determines your outlook.
Your outlook determines your output.
Your output determines your future.

Make sure you feed your mind
with things that inspire you.

Read the greatest books, listen to the
motivational speeches, attend
the grand seminars.

Make sure what goes into your mind
is founded in excellence.

**Remember, you had a
PURPOSE
before anyone had an
OPINION.**

Stay the course. Your intentions,
goals and actions are set.

Don't give a moment's notice
to the squawking crows
that live only to hold others back.

Keep your purpose before you at all times.

If it doesn't matter for eternity, then it **REALLY DOESN'T MATTER.**

We are each hit daily with needs, actions and desires. Our minds are bombarded with "things" our entire lives.

We have to make sure that we keep the most important "thing" of eternity at the top of the list.

Don't limit your challenges.

Challenge your limits.

Challenges can be…. challenging. We place a negative connotation on them.

Stop seeing them as an issue and start pushing your limits to be better.

If we don't teach our children who God is, someone else will teach them who He isn't.

Don't leave the education of your children to others.

Instill in them Godly principles.
Teach them the Word.
Write the Scripture on their heart.

I can guarantee you the world has a different view it is waiting to teach.

Better to have a small wedding and a
BIG MARRIAGE.

Today we spend thousands of dollars, hundreds of hours and an unlimited amount of stress in planning and holding weddings.

Conversely, very little time is spent planning a marriage.

Remember, the marriage will last an infinitely longer time than the wedding will.

A Bible falling apart usually belongs to someone who isn't.

Reading the Word and feeding upon it
is the path to success in life.

We can all read. Otherwise, what are you
doing with this book without pictures?
Reading is easy to do. Easy to do is defined
as something we can do.

The problem with easy to do is that it is also
easy not to do. DO THE EASY THING!

Become an OVERCOMER
or
become OVERCOME.

Tackle defeat. Rise from the ashes.
Push back.

To do otherwise places you in
the path of destruction.

He was as useless as the G in lasagna.

Stop laughing.
Better yet, stop pointing…. LOL

**Ability is what you
are capable of doing.
Motivation determines
what you do.
Attitude determines
how well you do it.**

Keep your attitude high,
your motivation strong and you will be
capable of more than you can imagine.

You don't have to see the whole staircase. Just take the first step.

If you will simply get started,
things change immediately.

You don't have to know everything;
just know you have to start.

On applications when the question is asked, "Who do you call in case of emergency?", I always put…. An Ambulance.

I'll just leave that one right here…. LOL

The problems we face today are here because the number of people who work for a living are now outnumbered by those who vote for a living.

Can I get an AMEN?

Have you ever noticed that the two words "The IRS" when put together spell THEIRS?

I know they believe it is. Don't believe me, just try to keep what you think is yours and see how soon they come to take what they think is theirs.… LOL

**At birth, you look like
your parent.
At death, you look like
your choices.
Choose wisely!**

Our lives are a series of choices.
Every choice matters. Every choice has
consequences…some good, some not.

Choose perfection. Choose greatness.

**You don't need a certain number of friends.
Just a number of friends you can be certain of.**

Surround yourself with people of honor and integrity. People that love you and only want the best for you.

It doesn't matter the quantity of people that fit that description. What matters is the quality of people that fit that description.

Life is like an elevator. On your way up, sometimes you have to stop and let some people off.

Not everyone will grow with you in life.

When you are changing for the better, there will be some that will not enjoy this process.

Let them go.

Those who are rowing the boat won't be rocking it.

Idle people stir the water. When you are busy, you don't have time for trouble.

If you have employees, keeping them busy will deter rocking the boat.

Don't fake it until you make it.

Face it until you make it.

Show up. Work hard. Fail. Get up.

Show up. Work hard. Fail. Get up.

Repeat.

Keep moving forward.

It's my wife's birthday tomorrow and she has been leaving jewelry magazines all over the house. So I bought her a magazine rack.

Men don't try this at home…. LOL

Some people are like slinkies. They aren't good for much but bring a smile to your face when pushed down the stairs.

I know, I know. Just kidding. But you will have to admit, it's funny.

Change the way you look at things and the things you look at change.

Perspective is key in life. We all have a perspective of many different angles, and most are founded in our experience.

To change your perspective,
you must change your input and actions.
When you change, things change.

Sometimes you have to hug people you don't like just so you'll know how big to dig the hole in the backyard.

Come on now, you know that's funny!

Rich people stay rich by living like they're broke.

Broke people stay broke by living like they're rich.

Study money. If you don't understand money, then it's likely you will never have any regardless of your income level.

When your out-go exceeds your income then your upkeep will be your downfall.

It will never matter how much money you make in life.

What matters in life is how much you keep.

Read like your success depends on it.

It does! Always be reading. Become such a dedicated reader that you will read the back of a cereal box if that is all that is around.

A smart person knows what to say.
A wise person knows whether to say it or not.

Momma always said,
"Think before you speak."

When our tongue outruns our mind,
we find ourselves in the ditch.

Whoever is trying to bring you down is already below you.

Don't walk away from these folks…RUN!

People who love you will never focus
on bringing you down.

**Some talk to you
in their free time.
Some free their time
to talk to you.
Know the difference.**

People who have your best interest at heart
will focus on you. While we read this and
think of others, we should apply it to
ourselves as well.

When you are arguing with a fool, make sure he isn't doing the same thing.

Words are powerful. Emotions are powerful.
When mixed incorrectly, the outcome
can become disastrous.

Do your best to make sure you keep
a level head and pure heart.

Chief cause of failure is trading what you want MOST for what you want NOW.

Discipline and telling yourself "No" will take you toward your goals in the most expedient manner.

Never trade the temporary for the permanent.

When prayer becomes your habit, miracles become your lifestyle.

Spend time daily in prayer. Practice it.
Be disciplined about it.

When you invest time talking to God
your return will exceed anything
this world can offer.

People are worried about what kind of planet we are leaving for our kids. Perhaps we should be worrying about what kind of kids we are leaving for our planet.

The greatest book tells us to "train up a child in the way he should go." That directive is not talking to the school, friends, neighbors, or relatives. While they are all important and play a role, it's talking about me as a parent.

Even perfect people buy pencils with erasers.

Not every idea will work. Not every effort
will pay off the way we expect.

When something doesn't "pan out"
the way we think it should,
take your eraser out and start over.

The only people who make money work at the mint.

Everyone else has to earn it.

Be diligent in your work. Teach your children the benefit of a good work ethic. Take pride in your work ethic.

Working is labor of love in motion.

**You have to gain skill.
Skill can be learned.
After all, your kids were
generated through
unskilled labor.**

Invest in learning. Whatever it is you are
doing in life, learn more about it.
Put what you learn into practice.

Strive to always be increasing your skill.

**Talent is God-given.
Be humble.**

**Fame is people-given.
Be grateful.**

**Conceit is self-given.
Be careful.**

Know the difference between all three.

Worry is a down payment on a problem you may never have.

Worrying profits nothing. When worrying arises, working is the best cure.

When you find yourself starting to worry, stand up, step up and start working.
You will find that the more you work the less you worry.

Our checkbooks and datebooks are true barometers of our heart condition.

It doesn't matter how we feel, what objectives we talk about, or what we believe in our minds to be true.

What matters is where our actions are taking us. Don't say that "family is the most important thing in my life" and have your calendar and checkbook prove you wrong.

**Families are like fudge…
mostly sweet with a few nuts!**

If you look around and see that everyone is sweet, you may be the nut…. LOL

Remember the 6 W's
Work Will Win
When Wishing Won't.

Nothing beats work.
Nothing generates success like work.

The most important things in life aren't things.

Can I get an amen? It's too sad when losing one of the truly important things is the time we realize this truth.

Most people will never run hard enough and far enough to ever see if they have that second wind or not.

Have you ever run a race and just when you think you can go no farther, you get that "second wind"?

Life, success, and overcoming all depend on the fact that you keep running.

Some people are like clouds, when they disappear it's a brighter day.

You don't need people in your life who are
always complaining, always negative.

Surround yourself with those
who see the sunshine.

The fact that there is a Highway to Hell and a Stairway to Heaven speaks loudly of expected traffic patterns.

Now that's good preaching and we all know it. Make sure you are on the right path.

When you are dead you don't know you are dead.

It's only difficult for others.

It's the same when you are stupid.

Mic drop!

BOAT – Bust Out Another Thousand
FAIL – First Attempt At Learning
END – Effort Never Dies
LUCK – Laboring Under Correct Knowledge.

More to come. I love a good acronym.

Hustle so hard your haters will be asking if you are hiring.

People see it when you are at maximum effort.

People are drawn to someone exerting that effort to move forward.

Be that person.

Good things are not cheap.

Cheap things are seldom good.

Never settle for anything less than the best.

Never give anything of yourself but the best.

You were not put here to make money.

You were put here to make a difference.

The question is which are you doing the most of?

**Don't look for a partner
who is eye candy.**

**Look for a partner
who is soul food.**

Choose wisely. One will fade with time.
The other will multiply.

When you follow the herd, you eventually end up at the slaughterhouse.

The masses are very seldom headed in the right direction.

Walk your own path…. but make sure daily it is the straight and narrow one.

Develop a backbone instead of a wishbone.

Stand up for what you believe in.

Nobody follows a wishbone individual.

If you're with the wrong people and are asking the wrong questions, you're wasting your time. If you're with the right people and are asking the right questions, you're investing your time.

The difference is staggering.
Look around and see who you are with.

What kills a skunk is the publicity it gives itself.

The only whale that gets a harpoon is the one that comes to the surface and blows.

Nobody likes a braggard!

Silence is golden.

Duct tape is silver.

Hey hey…. that's good and you know it…LOL

**Only as high as I reach
can I grow.
Only as far as I seek
can I go.
Only as deep as I look
can I see.
Only as much as I dream
can I be.**

Dream big!

My wife told me to grow up. It's hard to say anything when you have 45 gummy bears in your mouth.

You know you laughed.

If you're going to fight, fight like you're the third monkey on the ramp to Noah's Ark and it's starting to rain.

When you decide to do something, go all in. If it is worth doing, then it is worth putting all of your effort and focus into.

Start, work and don't give up.

I sent that ancestry site some information on my family tree.

They sent me a packet of seeds and suggested I start over.

We can change our mind, but we can't change our family. Whether your ancestry is awesome or leaves a bit to be desired, this has nothing to do with you.
Write your own story.

**My dad would swear
and always say,
"Excuse my French."**

**One day the teacher asked if
anyone knew a foreign
language and I raised my hand.**

Be careful of what you say, little ears are
listening…and repeating.

Let your speech be filled with wisdom,
honor and positive life-giving words.

First you Learn.

Then you remove the "L"

Rarely in life does your financial health increase prior to you taking time to learn.

We are blessed to have so many avenues today to learn from.

Wealthy people typically have big libraries in their homes. Financially panicked people typically have big TVs.

Some things to ponder:

What happens if get scared to death twice?

They're not going to make yardsticks any longer.

Went to the air and space museum but there was nothing there.

If attacked by a mob of clowns, go for the juggler.

More things to ponder:

The past, present and future walk into a bar. It was tense.

**Practice safe eating.
Use condiments.**

The first 5 days of a weekend are the hardest.

I childproofed my house, but the kids still get in.

If you're going to be a bear,

Be a grizzly.

My best friend Rick Ferguson says this all the time.

What he means is that if you are going to do something, go all in. Go big. Go great.

Do it all. Enjoy it all.

Things are never going to change…. until you change.

The circumstances you find yourself in, your current place in life, and the people surrounding you. All of these and many more are a blessing or an issue.

Don't catch yourself complaining about any of them. They will remain the way they are as long as you remain the way you are.

We must change. Start today. Change can start with simply changing what we put into our minds. Read a great book. (I know, you are reading a good one right now.)

To truly change everything around us, the change must start with us.

How long should you try?

UNTIL

How long should you work
on your success in life? Until.
How long should you work
on improving your health? Until.
How long should you invest time into your
relationships for them to change? Until.
How long should you work
on your dreams?
UNTIL
Until success is yours, you continue to work.

The challenge of leadership is to
Be strong, but not rude
Be kind, but not weak
Be bold, but not a bully
Be thoughtful, but not lazy
Be humble, but not timid
Be proud, but not arrogant
Have humor, but without folly

A delicate balance and attention to detail is required by all leaders. Doing this will ensure that your followers will be your biggest supporters.

Success is nothing more than a few simple disciplines, practiced every day. While failure is simply a few errors in judgment, repeated every day.

It is the accumulative weight of our disciplines and our judgments that leads us to either fortune or failure.

Let others lead small lives and
accomplish small things....
But not you.

Let others argue over small
things and small events....
But not you.

Let others cry over small hurts
and disappointments....
But not you.

Let others leave their fortunes
in someone else's hands....
But not you.

**If you wish to find,
you must search.**

**Rarely does a good idea
interrupt you.**

The Greatest Book says that if a person seeks, they will find. Seeking means taking action. Seeking means working. Seeking means focusing.

Start your search today.

Blowing out someone else's candles doesn't make yours shine brighter.

There are two ways to have the tallest building in town:
1. Tear all the others down.
2. Build your own.

Be a builder.

**You don't get
what you wish for.**

You get what you work for.

Working always wins when wishing won't.

It's great to set goals, plans, wishes, dreams and everything that goes with it. The one difference-making ingredient is ACTION.

Action is the term we use for WORK.

Life is too short to leave the keys to your happiness in someone else's pocket.

Happiness is an inside job. The truth is that most of us are as happy as we intend to be.

Yes, I said it. Your happiness is up to you, and it is your responsibility.

Take responsibility today for your happiness.

There is only one book that you can read that no matter where you are, what you are doing, who you are with, what you have done or where you are going, when you read it, the author is watching.

The Greatest Book has the ability to transform your life. Just imagine that each time you pick it up and read it, the author is watching you take in every word.

I don't know about you, but that is humbling.

Don't let anyone rent space in your head unless they are a good tenant.

We spend too much time in our lives worrying about what other people think of us. They take up space in our heads.

Make sure that anyone you have allowed into your mind is pushing you toward greatness.

Honesty is a very expensive gift. Don't expect it from cheap people…. Warren Buffet

You'll never get ahead of anyone as long as you try to get even with him…. Lou Holtz

Price is what you pay, value is what you get…. Warren Buffet

If you are in a dark place and think you are buried, you need to see that you have been planted…. Mark Turner

Changing your perspective is key to changing your circumstances.

When life has performed an avalanche on you, stop, breathe and understand it is simply another place to start from.

If you don't heal what hurts you, you will bleed on people that didn't cut you.

There is another saying that goes like this: "Hurting people hurt people".

When we are hurting, we have a tendency to lash out. We typically lash out at those we love the most and who are closest to us.

Understand that we need to assess our hurt, be honest about what is hurting us and address the source. Doing this will avoid damaged relationships.

**Doing what is right
is not always popular.**

**Doing what is popular
isn't always right.**

Regardless of the direction of the masses,
always do what is right.

Do what is right when everyone around you
is telling you to do something different.

Doing what is right will maintain your
integrity.

Small boys become big men through the influence of big men who care about small boys.

For you dads and grandads out there, invest time in young men. The same goes for little girls and women.

The Greatest Book says to train up a child in the way they should go.

If you don't train them and invest time in them, the world certainly will.

When you ask God why He is taking you through rough waters, remember, it is because He knows your enemies can't swim.

Often, we don't understand why the storms of life pummel us. When we focus on the storm and the problems we are experiencing, it can be overwhelming. We question Why.

Understand that we don't always see the larger plan. Understand that we don't usually have all the answers. Understand and have faith that the One that does, knows what He is doing.

God is trying to write your story…. stop stealing the pen.

I told my wife to embrace her mistakes…. she hugged me.

I'm going to stand outside so if anyone asks…. I'm outstanding!

I was wondering why the Frisbee was getting bigger…. and then it hit me.

Today I saw an ad that said, "radio for sale, $1, volume stuck on full." I thought to myself, "I can't turn that down."

Two silkworms challenged each other to a race. It ended in a tie.

England has no kidney bank, but it does have a Liverpool.

Haunted French pancakes give me the crepes.

**The state you find yourself in is
your condition,
not your conclusion.**

Remember:

**There are no accidents.
You were uniquely designed
and created. It's up to you
what that creation becomes.**

All your customers are partners in your mission.... Shep Hyken

The best way to find yourself is to lose yourself in the service of others.... Mahatma Gandhi

Always render more and better service than expected of you, no matter what your task may be.... Og Mandino

Leadership is service, not position.... Tim Fargo

We take photos of everything today but fail to capture the moment.

A recently released report told the story of tourists visiting the edge of the Grand Canyon.

Tourist after tourist walked to the edge and used their phones to take pictures of the beauty of the canyon.

Stepping back, they gathered in groups looking at their phones.

With the grandeur of one of the most magnificent creations right before them, they were lost in their phone.

Capture the moment. **BE WHERE YOUR FEET ARE.**

Gratitude begins when your sense of entitlement ends.

Gratitude is said to be one of the greatest "tudes" that exists. However, when we begin to feel we are entitled our gratitude level falls.

Be grateful in everything…both good and bad. You can rejoice in the good and learn from the bad.

Don't let your ice cream melt while you are counting someone else's sprinkles.

Every one of us is gifted with talents.
Utilizing them is a choice.

Don't get caught saying,
"If I just had the ability to do what that person does, or if I just had that talent, what great things I could do."

The plain truth is that if you are not using the gifts and talents you have been given, you would not use someone else's either.

Rejoice in who you are and the talents you were given. Don't compare to others….
grow in yours.

Your speech is your heart on display to the world.

Your words and how you use them tell the world where your heart is.

Listening to them, would someone discern you to be good or evil?

Don't be lazy in your speech. People who use a multitude of four-letter words have a limited vocabulary. Learn new words.

I had a dream about mufflers.
I woke up exhausted.

To write with a broken pencil
is pointless.

I stayed up all night wondering
where the sun had gone.
Then it dawned on me!

Ability is what you are capable of doing.

Motivation determines what you do.

Attitude determines how well you do it.

Make sure you have your attitude set on the positive.

You will never achieve your goals if you continue to exchange what you want most for what you want today.

The temporary, or NOW, can get in the way of the GREAT.

Don't allow the desire for things or activities that seem so appealing today to derail your goals.

Great goals and great achievements take time. Stay the course.

People live in four different time zones:

Spare Time
Part Time
Full Time
All Time

Success in life lies within living in the All Time Zone.

My grandfather always said,
"When one door closes
another one opens."
He was a wonderful man.
Terrible cabinet maker.

Wanna get back on your feet?
Just miss a couple of
car payments.

A bicycle can't stand alone.
It's just two tired.

A will is a dead giveaway.

A dentist and a manicurist married. They fought tooth and nail. (Great dad joke)

I got some batteries that were given out free of charge.

Did you hear about the fellow whose entire left side was cut off? He's all right now.

He had a photographic memory, but it was never fully developed.

A thief stole a calendar. He got twelve months.

Acupuncture is a jab well done. That's the point.

When you get a bladder infection, urine trouble.

When chemists die, they barium.

I'm reading a book about anti-gravity. I can't put it down.

**What one person receives
without working for,
another person must work
without receiving.**

Understand this, there is no "Free Lunch"
Somebody pays.

Work is a God-given ability for
every person on the earth. The Greatest
Book states that those who don't
work shouldn't eat.

Don't be a receiver without being a giver.

The government cannot give to anybody anything that the government must first take from someone else.

When we hear that the government is giving "free money" to people under whatever reason they provide, just know they took it from other people to start with.

During the pandemic when the checks from the government were flowing, that money came from the pockets of working Americans – many of whom received no check.

Don't fall victim to thinking the government is your guidance or financial counselor.

Your mind will always believe everything you tell it.

Feed it hope.

Feed it truth.

Feed it with love.

You don't go to the next level until you grow to the next level.

Investing in yourself is the fastest way to advance in your career or chosen endeavor.

Most people stop learning the moment they leave school. This one action determines those who rise to greatness and those who don't.

Never stop learning. Invest in yourself.

Sometimes you meet someone, and you know right then you want to spend your whole life without them.

They can brighten an entire room, simply by leaving.

Laughter is like a windshield wiper – it doesn't stop the rain but allows us to keep going.

I bought my wife a refrigerator for her birthday. Man, you should've seen her face light up when she opened it up.

It's better to train your employees and have them leave, than not training them and have them stay.

I always hear business owners say, "What if I invest in training them and they leave?" The better question is, "What if I don't train them and they stay?"

Put a high priority on training your people. You will not regret it.

Invest more in yourself than you do your career.

Personal growth comes before professional growth.

Take that course. Buy that book. Spend time at that weekend seminar.

When you grow personally, everything grows around you.

**Success is when you
add value to yourself.**

**Significance is when you
add value to others.**

Strive, as best you can,
to live a life of significance.

Adding to the value of other people's lives
will in turn add immense value to yours.

The best thing a person can hear is someone
saying, "Let me tell you the difference this
person made in my life."

The smartest, healthiest and wisest people in the world choose education over entertainment. The most unsuccessful, unhealthy, unwealthy, and unwise people choose entertainment over education.

Choose wisely every day.

I don't know one person that leaves their cart in the middle of the parking lot.

If you are too big to do the small things, then you are too small to do the big things.

Success lies in doing the small things. The easy things are the route to greatness.

The only problem with doing the easy things is they are also easy not to do.

Do the easy things!

The shadows will always be behind you when you are walking toward the light.

Make certain your steps are leading
you toward the best.

Never take your eyes off the great,
and never settle for the good
when the great is ahead.

Walking toward the light means you
understand what is important and valuable
and that all troubles will be in your wake.

There are four types of wealth:
  1. **Financial Wealth (money)**
  2. **Social Wealth (status)**
  3. **Time Wealth (freedom)**
  4. **Physical Wealth (health)**

Be wary of the job that lures you with 1 and 2 and robs you of 3 and 4.

Be honest with yourself and stay true to your path. Never sacrifice your freedom or health for money or status.

Staying positive does not mean things will turn out OK.

It means you will be OK no matter how things turn out.

I cannot stress enough how important a positive attitude is.

Will it make everything better? No

However, it will make everything better than a negative attitude will.

Nothing will kill a great employee faster than watching you tolerate a bad one.

Tolerating bad performance, bad attitude
and bad actors is the mark of bad leadership.

Take action immediately or the only
employees you will have left
are the bad ones.

An arrow can only be shot by pulling it backwards.

When life is dragging you back with difficulties, it means it's going to launch you into something great.

So, just keep focusing and aiming.

Use the trial of life as a springboard to success.

Life isn't designed to give you what you need. It is designed to give you what you deserve.

Input equals outcome.

You should not believe you should receive a harvest if you haven't worked the soil and planted good seeds.

Don't get caught in the
"I deserve" category. Place yourself in the
"I have deposited" category.

No farmer ever received a crop
he did not first plant.

People will forgive you for being the leader you should be, but they will not forgive you for being the leader you claim to be.

Be authentic. Don't put on haughty shows.
Don't try to be the tough guy,
the strict one, the dictator. It never flies.

Show people how much you care.
Apologize when you make a mistake.

Just because they are in your circle doesn't mean they are in your corner.

Surround yourself with people you know,
within a shadow of a doubt,
that are in your corner.

Look at the five people closest to you in this life. Make certain they are in your corner.

If you rearrange the letters in
DEPRESSION
You get
I PRESSED ON

The Bible is full of Freaks,
Frauds and Failures and
He uses them all.

If people treat you like
an option, leave them like
a choice.

Sometimes we have to let go
of what's killing us even
if it is killing us to let go.

When Eagles are silent, parrots begin to chatter…. Winston Churchill

Don't complain.
Eighty percent of the people you complain to don't care and the other twenty percent are glad you have problems….
Lou Holtz

The unknown is easier to face when you have a hand to hold…. Mark Turner

When you realize how much you are truly worth, you will stop giving people discounts.

The Greatest Book says that you are fearfully and wonderfully made.

The moment you realize exactly what that means you will have an insight most people never grasp.

Don't hang around people that don't treat you like the jewel that you are.

When you enter His presence with praise, He enters your presence with power.

Show your praise to God every day.

Let's be honest, there is no way to get through this life without holding the hand of the Almighty.

Rest in his power by showing Him your praise.

**The devil knows your name
and calls you by your sin.**

**God knows your sin and calls
you by your name.**

It doesn't get much more powerful than this.

Dwell on this for a bit.

Don't say God is silent when your Bible is closed.

**God has a tendency
of picking up a nobody
to be somebody
in front of everybody
without consulting anybody.**

He has chosen you!

P.E.A.C.E. – Putting Everything Aside Claim Eternity

F.A.I.T.H. – Finding Answers In Trusting Him

L.O.V.E. – Let Our Voices Encourage

H.O.P.E. – Hold On, Pain Ending

It is my sincerest prayer that God blesses each of you greatly and that your lives are lived to the fullest extent possible.

About the Author

Mark Turner is the CEO of N2Success, a professional speaking, training and consulting firm. His expertise is in the field of management stemming from his 35+ years in the corporate world.

Mark is the former Chief Operating Officer and President of Value-Added Communications where he grew the company 3,750% in 11 years.

Mark was one of the first people chosen out of a large number of international applicants by the Zig Ziglar Corporation to be a Ziglar Certified Speaker and Trainer.

He is also certified by Dr. Robert Rohm in the Model of Human Behavior and incorporates these modalities in his leadership series.

Mark has served as the Mayor of his hometown, Wills Point, Texas, for over 10 years. He has served the Boy Scouts of America as a Scoutmaster, Cubmaster and is Wood Badge Certified.

Mark believes, like Zig Ziglar, that you can have everything you want in life by simply helping enough other people get what they want. He is a public servant and utilizes his heart of service wherever needed.

Mark is married to his wife of 43 years Cathy, and they reside in Wills Point. They have two children, Grant and Katie who with their spouses Chia and Dusty have four grandchildren – Maverick, Cora Belle, Serafina and Juniper. Mark says they don't call them "grand" for nothing.

You can contact Mark at:
mark@n2success.com
www.n2success.com

Disclaimer & Copyright Information

The author and publisher have made every effort to ensure that the information in this book was correct at press time. The author and publisher do not assume and hereby disclaim any liability to any party for any loss, damage, or disruption caused by errors or omissions, whether such errors or omissions result from negligence, accident, or any other cause.

All quotes, unless otherwise noted, are attributed to the author.
Cover illustration, book design and production by
www.TributePublishing.com
Copyright © 2023

www.ingramcontent.com/pod-product-compliance
Lightning Source LLC
Chambersburg PA
CBHW020534080526
44583CB00013B/855